READY
TO
WORK
WORKBOOK

**What You Need to Know
Before Your Next Interview**

LISA SUMMEROUR ED.D.

AUTHOR: **Lisa Summerour, Ed.D.**
COVER DESIGN: **Clean Sweep Publishing**
EDITING: **Clean Sweep Publishing**
FORMATTING: **Officeworx**

Printed in the United States of America.

ISBN: 978-1-7340972-9-0

Clean Sweep Publishing

ACKNOWLEDGMENTS

I am a proud graduate of what is now Riverside University High School, Milwaukee, Wisconsin. The business education classes, and work experience I gained as a high school student, laid an incredible foundation for my professional career.

I want to thank my late grandmother, Mrs. Margaret (Pinkett) Magruder for modeling what job readiness looked like. Seeing her finish college in 1973 as a married woman with six children was miraculous. She was the only black student in her nursing degree program, and she graduated at the top of her class. She went on to run an ambulatory center managing a budget that exceeded one million dollars. She taught me to keep my eyes on the possibilities because anything was possible.

Finally, everyone should have an accountability team. I am so thankful for the guidance and empowerment I receive from my accountability alliance. Kath Schnorr and Dr. Gail Whitaker, thank you. Our weekly sessions mean the world to me.

DEDICATION

You are demonstrating what it takes to create more and better opportunities for yourself. Your ability to learn, grow, and transform into your best self will provide inspiration for someone else to pursue their goals. My prayer is that the Get Ready to Work Workbook empowers you to embrace the job search process and to walk confidently into your next position.

The Get Ready to Work Workbook is dedicated to you because, without knowing you personally, you were on my mind the entire time I was putting it together.

This is for you!

Table of Contents

Introduction

I wrote the Get Ready to Work Workbook for several reasons. First, as a tool to help individuals who don't typically have access to professional resources and those who don't know where to find career advancement or job readiness information. I want to help people develop confidence whether they are looking for work or pursuing an entrepreneurial passion. Either way, your ability to present yourself well and communicate effectively will be crucial to your ability to establish healthy networking relationships.

The Get Ready to Work Workbook is a resource that can help three specific groups of people:

- Students in high school and college.

- Individuals returning to the workforce:

    o   After being incarcerated

    o   After being in the military

    o   After taking time off to be home

- Individuals who feel their interviewing skills need updating.

The Get Ready to Work Workbook is designed to be used alone, worked through as part of a training program or course requirement, or used in tandem with a book I co-authored entitled "The 4-Tions: Your Guide to Developing Successful Job Search Strategies." The 4-Tions provides many technical aspects of the job search, and I highly recommend adding it to your library. the Get Ready to Work Workbook addresses information in greater detail, includes information on networking and public speaking, and provides information on several types of interviews with which you should become familiar. the Get Work Workbook is a book and workbook combined, and it is designed to help you better understand the information on a more personal level.

The Get Read to Work Workbook is needed to help you do two things. First, I wanted it to be interactive, so your engagement can empower you. Second, I needed to provide some of the why's behind what you will learn. Being told what you should do is one thing. Your understanding of why it's important for you – that is a huge takeaway. My desire is that you complete each section and gain a deeper understanding of why that section was necessary to you. Personalizing the information is key to finding practical ways to apply what you learn so you are empowered to move forward with real data.

To that end, your contribution to making the Get Ready to Work Workbook work for you involves you gaining clarity around three things:

1. Believe there is something unique about you and acknowledge that what you have to offer will never be seen by the world if you don't identify it, nurture it, and put it into action.

2. Identify your gifts, talents, and the things you are good at and passionate about doing.

3. Understand why it benefits you to embrace the process of developing your confidence so that you can apply numbers 1 and 2 wholeheartedly, consistently, and on purpose.

I desire that you learn useful information in the Get Ready to Work Workbook that you can refer to for years to come. If you engage in learning this information and practicing the processes reviewed in the text, I believe you can be better prepared for:

- Job interviews

- Meetings

- Client prospecting

- Public presentations for work, school, or social events

- Professional interactions

- Networking opportunities

Whether you're reading the Get Ready to Work Workbook because someone gave it to you, you purchased a copy; it is required reading for a course, workshop, training, or – you found it lying around and picked it up - you are into it this far so you might as well take advantage of this resource. Please read it, work through it, and apply what you learn. Then, go back to areas for refreshers whenever necessary. You might want to copy some pages before using them so you will have them to reuse over and over again. You can also visit the Get Ready to Work Workbook page at www.liveempoweredinstitute.com where some pages are available for download.

Clarifying why you believe the Get Ready to Work Workbook can help you will be an essential component in keeping you motivated. You may have things in your life or from your past that have left you feeling inadequate, ill-equipped, disadvantaged, or confused about how to present yourself in a positive, personable and professional manner. Asking yourself questions like, "Why am I here?" and "Why am I using the Get Ready to Work Workbook?" will help you identify the purpose. Purpose enables you to align your behavior to something meaningful.

Now, let's get to work!

You can begin by answering the following questions:

Why am I using the Get Ready to Work Workbook or Why am I taking this workshop?

Avoid answers like; *to get a job* or *because I have to*. Dig deeper. Consider questions like; who are you doing this to help? Whose lives will you positively impact as a result of changing your life? What purpose do you want to fulfill?

_____

_____

_____

_____

_____

_____

_____

_____

_____

_____

_____

_____

_____

_____

_____

_____

_____

_____

_____

_____

_____

_____

_____

_____

What am I afraid of, or most concerned about as I begin the Get Ready to Work Workbook, this course or workshop?

_____

_____

_____

_____

_____

_____

_____

_____

_____

_____

_____

_____

_____

_____

_____

_____

_____

_____

_____

_____

_____

_____

_____

_____

_____

_____

What do I hope to gain or achieve by completing the Get Ready to Work Workbook?

_____

_____

_____

_____

_____

_____

_____

_____

_____

_____

_____

_____

_____

_____

_____

_____

_____

_____

_____

_____

_____

_____

_____

_____

_____

_____

_____

Attitude vs. Character

> "Attitude is Everything!"
> ~ Keith Harrell

Attitude is extremely important. We sometimes confuse attitude and character without knowing it. Attitude and character can be aligned or misaligned. So, what's the difference?

Attitude

One way of thinking about it is your attitude is *how you choose to respond* to a specific situation or person, in a given moment. Your attitude is what you present to others. It could include facial expressions, tone of voice, even sounds you make when you aren't actually speaking.

Character

Is connected to identify. You may have heard of the phrase character traits. Character traits can be positive or negative. Generally, character describe aspects about you that are central to you as a person. Character is *what guides you even when no one is watching*.

Is it possible to be known as a person of good character, and still demonstrate a bad attitude? If you think "yes" how might that look?

_____

_____

_____

_____

Can you give an example of someone known to have bad character, who has a good attitude?

_____

_____

_____

We are going to focus on character. More specifically, you are going to focus on your character strengths. What are your Character Strengths? What do you believe are some of your Character Strengths?

_____

_____

_____

_____

Would you like to find out about your Character Strengths so you can understand how they help you engage others?

Visit viacharacter.org to take the FREE Character Strengths Assessment.

The VIA Character Strengths Survey

Get to know your greatest strengths.

Why take the survey?

The VIA Survey is the only free, scientific survey of character strengths in the world. Take this simple, 15 minute character test and discover your greatest strengths. Research shows that knowing and using your character strengths can help you:

✓ Increase happiness and well-being

✓ Find meaning and purpose

✓ Boost relationships

✓ Manage stress and health

✓ Accomplish goals

What are your top three Character Strengths and how are they described?

1. _____

_____

2. _____

_____

3. _____

_____

What do you think about these three Character Strengths?

1. _____

   _____

2. _____

   _____

3. _____

   _____

Can you recall times when these three Character Strengths have shown up in your life? If so, how?

1. _____

   _____

2. _____

   _____

3. _____

   _____

Danette was off to a rough start. She woke up late and spilled coffee on her blouse, rushing to get out of the apartment. Because Danette hadn't made a test run to the interview location, she got lost getting to the building. She pulled into what looked like a full parking lot and spotted a space in the next aisle. She sped up to get around to that aisle. Another car pulled in and took the one empty slot in the row as she got closer. Out of frustration, Danette honked her horn. It got the woman's attention, and there was a brief moment of awkward eye contact between them as Danette drove by visibly frustrated. Danette found a parking spot in the lot next door. With further to walk, she grabbed her purse and quickly headed to the building next door. She arrived at the reception desk frazzled and clearly not at her best.

Kimberly, the receptionist, could see that Danette was not having a good morning. Kimberly had Danette sign-in and pointed to show her the waiting area. Then Kimberly said, "You still have a few minutes before your interview. If you need to go to the restroom, it's down the hall to the right."

Danette sighed and mouthed the words "thank you" to Kimberly as she headed toward the restroom. Great, she thought, I can get in there and refocus. First, Danette took a good look in the mirror and got herself pulled back together. The coffee stain was there but not visible as long as her jacket was closed. All things considered, Danette didn't look nearly as frazzled as she was feeling.

She took a few deep breaths, looked in the mirror again, and whispered to herself, "You are qualified for this position, and you are prepared for this interview. You got this!" She checked to be sure her cellphone was off. She made sure she had copies of her resume and the correct forms of identification if anyone wanted copies. Then, she closed her eyes and said a prayer. When she opened her eyes, she looked back into the mirror, and she was finally able to smile. Danette headed back out to the waiting area. William, the HR Admin, greeted her a short time later to escort her to her first interview.

Danette felt good as she turned into the doorway, looked across the office, and saw the Director of Human Resources, Ms. Mattilyn Rochester. She recognized her immediately. Ms. Rochester was the woman she honked at for "stealing" her parking space less than an hour ago.

If you were Danette, what would you do or say at this moment? Use one or more of the three Character Strengths you shared to create a response for Danette. Keep it realistic and have fun with it. It's your story to tell!

_____

_____

_____

_____

_____

_____

_____

_____

_____

_____

_____

_____

_____

_____

_____

_____

_____

_____

_____

_____

_____

_____

_____

Danette froze. It all happened in an instant. Her feelings of fear, disappointment, and shame converged, and she froze. She gathered herself quickly and said, "Hi, I'm the frantic, horn honking woman in the parking lot who was desperately trying to be early for her interview." She followed immediately with, "I am so sorry. I must have seemed rude and inconsiderate. I promise you that behavior was out of character for me." She extended her hand, "Hi, I'm Danette Pinkett."

Perhaps it was her sincerity that came through. Maybe it was the fact that Ms. Rochester had been doing this long enough not to be surprised that a candidate might become frustrated trying to find parking in their always crowded parking lot. Whatever the reason, Ms. Rochester extended her hand, welcomed Danette into her office, and they went on to have a good interview.

Are you wondering if Danette got the job? Who knows?

What matters is Danette found a way to recover from a less than flattering situation. Were her superpowers her Character Strengths? One of her top Character Strengths was Humor, which she used immediately to lighten the situation. Another Character Strength was Bravery, which she needed to apologize, hold her head up, and maintain confidence as she moved through her interview.

Would you have been as cool, calm and collected as Danette? Would you have responded as gracefully as Ms. Rochester?

_____

_____

_____

_____

Notes

_____

_____

_____

_____

_____

_____

_____

_____

Wardrobe and Appearance

Society, traditions, peer pressure, office dress codes, and other factors can influence what we wear and when. When it comes to an interview, do not assume you should automatically know the dress code for every potential work environment. It isn't possible. However, **it is your responsibility to know *what, when*, and *why* about *wardrobe* for your interview.** How will you learn? Ask.

Today, the rules can change considerably from one place to the next. In this business casual age, some environments once known for strict dress codes have adapted; allowing employees to wear jeans even if it's only on dress down Friday. That means what you wear to a job interview could be influenced by the day of the week! It is your responsibility to pay attention to the one opportunity you get to make a great first impression. Putting thought and effort into your wardrobe in advance will help you prepare for when it's essential and waiting until the last minute could set you up for disappointment.

What might the challenges be when trying to dress appropriately for an interview?

1. _____

_____

2. _____

_____

3. _____

_____

4. _____

_____

5. _____

_____

Notes

_____

_____

_____

_____

Observe

What position do you see yourself interviewing for?

_____

_____

_____

_____

Do you feel you have what you need to dress appropriately for a job interview?

☐ Yes ☐ No

Use this list of items to determine if you think you could put an interview outfit together based upon what you currently have at home:

- Shoes (dress, sneaker, heel height, closed-toe, opened-toe, sandal, color)

- Jewelry (earrings, necklace, rings, nose / lip piercing, hair pin, bracelet)

- Perfume / cologne

- Hair (wig, weave, extensions, beard, mustache)

- Make-up (list all of the items you would wear for the interview, like foundation, powder, highlights, lipstick, eye shadow, blush, eyebrow pencil / powder, fake lashes (permanent or temporary and how long are they)

- Accessories (belt, purse, briefcase, notepad)

Use this chart as a guide to help you better understand dress code categories:

Item	Labor / Warehouse	Casual	Business Casual	Business
Sneaker	X			
Work Boot	X			
Casual Shoe	X	X		
Dress Shoe		X	X	
Uniform / Special Gear	X	X	X	
Polo Style	X	X	X	
Blouse / Dress Shirt		X	X	X
Jeans	X	X	X	
Skirt / Slacks		X	X	X
Sweater / Blazer		X	X	X
Suit			X	X
Tie				X

There are often exceptions and some overlap when it comes to how different organizations define dress codes. For example, some organizations might view jeans as part of their business casual dress code while others do not. Or, perhaps jeans are only permitted on "dress down" Friday at one company while another company allows jeans to be worn once a year at the company picnic. On the other hand, special gear could mean construction gear, a company uniform, or company logo wear that employees can wear any day of the week at one company but only permitted for special events at another company.

Hopefully, the guide will help you with a general understanding of the different dress code categories. It is better to err on the side of being dressed above the code rather than below the code. In other words, if you aren't sure about a Polo style shirt, wear the dress shirt or blouse. If you aren't sure about a suit for business casual, take the suit jacket along to put on if you want to dress up the shirt or blouse, you're already wearing. Carry a tie along in your jacket pocket or bag. If you need to make a quick wardrobe update to put it on – you will have what you need with you.

What are your thoughts, feelings, questions, or concerns about the section you just completed?

_____

_____

_____

_____

Do you know what you would wear to an interview? Do you have everything you need? If not, what's missing?

_____

_____

_____

_____

In this section, we will address some common concerns when it comes to dressing for an interview. It may seem like overkill but trust me when I tell you – each one of the items listed has created a problem for someone in preparing for a first impression opportunity. Each one of the items listed could be a distraction during your first impression opportunity.

The Goal

For you to end up with two complete outfits that are appropriate for the types of interviews or first impression opportunities you expect to experience.

Concern #1. I do not know the company dress code.

Addressing this one will help you streamline some of your other concerns. Even if you have a closet full of fabulous clothes, you could still end up dressing inappropriately for the interview if you do not know the dress code.

The way to get this information is to ask! Ask the person who contacted you about the interview. If you're going through an agency, ask your representative at the agency. You want to ask the question: _**What is the company or office dress code?**_

Do this for every interview. Do not assume that one company's dress code will be the same as another. Sometimes, dress codes change from one department to another within the same company.

Concern #2. I do not know how to put a wardrobe together based upon what's in my closet.

I do not want to minimize the importance of appearance. It is crucial, and it can be a real challenge. It may also be one of the more fun things you get to do during this process. Even though you may feel some angst around what you have or don't have in terms of wardrobe, decide to enjoy the process. Working on the intrinsic aspects of how you show up, like your attitude, will always be more important. Working on the external areas, how you look, can be a bit of a relief and allow you to show your personality before you even introduce yourself.

For this exercise – start gathering photographs from magazines, online sites, and even pictures you can take with your phone of store mannequins. See if you can put outfits in the categories listed in the chart on Page 18. Please keep it simple. Consider basics like a shirt, pants, and shoes. If you think it's necessary, add a tie and jacket. Remember to include socks and a belt when appropriate.

Concern #3. I have limited funds or no money available to purchase clothing for my interview or first impression opportunity.

It is so important to invest in yourself. Reading the Get Ready to Work Workbook is an investment. Taking a course or workshop to prepare for your job search, is an investment in your future. Being prepared for your interviews is yet another investment. Some investments require time, others attention, some money, and a few require a combination of all three!

If you can adjust your budget to set aside funds that build until you can afford to purchase a few items, that's great. However, that's not always possible, and sometimes you don't have time to "wait for your bank account to grow." In that instance, there are organizations and other things you may want to investigate as potential sources for obtaining suitable clothing for your interviews and first impression opportunities. They include:

- Friends or family members

- Organizations that provide free clothing for individuals preparing for interviews

- Stores that offer apparel sold at a discount:

  o Used clothing stores, thrift shops, Salvation Army, Goodwill

  o Outlet stores

You may need to be creative. Your outfits could come from combining items from these sources and mixing them with pieces you already have in your closet. When asking friends or family members, be prepared to hear "yes" and be ready to hear "no." Do not judge based on your assumption of what you think they have or what you think they "should" do for you. Everyone views clothing differently, and for some, loaning clothing is not comfortable. Both "yes" and "no" are acceptable answers because both let you know your options. Get the answer, thank the person, and move on.

Review / Assess

OK . . let's take a break and check-in using a short assessment. I'm going to ask you to separate your thoughts from your feelings as you answer the questions below.

What THOUGHTS come to mind as you think about asking friends and family to borrow clothing?

_____

_____

_____

What FEELINGS surfaced around asking friends and family about borrowing clothing?

_____

_____

_____

What THOUGHTS come to mind as you think about getting clothes from a charity or donation site?

_____

_____

_____

_____

What FEELINGS surfaced around getting clothing from a charity or donation site?

_____

_____

_____

_____

What THOUGHTS come to mind as you think about purchasing clothing from a thrift or discount store?

_____

_____

_____

_____

What FEELINGS surfaced around purchasing clothing from a thrift or discount store?

_____

_____

_____

_____

Did any uncomfortable feelings come over you as you worked through these questions? If not, fantastic! If so, here are your next questions:

Go to the **Why are you using the Get Ready to Work Workbook** section on Page 9 and review your reason(s).

Are your reasons for wanting to make a good first impression more important than your discomfort?

Is your unique purpose in life more important than your discomfort?

If your reasons are not powerful enough to move you through the discomfort of getting the wardrobe, you will need to make an excellent first impression, and it's OK to adjust your motivating factor; your WHY. The reasons you want to make changes in your life must be powerful enough to move you through EVERYTHING you will face on the path to achieving your goal.

How are you feeling about wearing the right outfit for an interview?

Why is it important to know what to wear to an interview?

_____

_____

_____

_____

How will wearing the right clothing make you feel?

_____

_____

_____

_____

What do you need to do to create one or two interview outfits?

    a.   What is missing in your wardrobe?

    b.   What do you need to change, update, or acquire?

_____

_____

_____

_____

Who can you ask for help?

_____

_____

_____

_____

Where can you go for help first?

_____

_____

_____

_____

Notes

_____

_____

_____

Grooming

This section includes often overlooked information. Whether you are reviewing the Get Ready to Work Workbook alone or in a facilitated session, please realize that this section may bring up uncomfortable feelings because it addresses aspects of us as individuals that often reflect our uniqueness. So, it might feel personal. This section may cause you to reflect on whether a favorite piece of jewelry, clothing, or fragrance is appropriate to wear to an interview or a new job. You may start wondering if it's time to change your hairstyle or shave your beard.

I wrote this book to help you present yourself in interviews and other first impression situations – in the best light possible. It's important that you still "feel like you." We can all think of cases where we changed our appearance without feeling like we compromised who we are as a person. How you show up to hang with friends may look different from how you want to show up at an interview. Keep that in mind as you move through this section.

The Get Ready to Work Workbook is about getting to work when it comes to your job search or starting your own business. It is also about working on yourself in other aspects, so you appear and feel ready!

Make your commitment to investing in yourself, all-inclusive. No shortcuts. No quick fixes. In the end, these are suggestions; things to consider. For some, they will be welcomed reminders! You will make the final decision on what you are willing to do in each interview situation. Let's get to work.

Skincare / Hygiene

Shower / Bath / Wash-Up

I would rather say it than not say it. Whether it's a shower, a bath, or you decide to wash-up in a basin – with some good ole' soap and water - be clean.

Tattoos

Self-expression through tattoos has become more prevalent than anyone probably could have imagined. Whether or not someone thinks tattoos are acceptable or not could depend heavily on your age, lifestyle, upbringing, your cultural associations, or a combination of these and other variables. Whether you are a budding entrepreneur or someone looking to be hired, you need to learn about the policies and expectations of the place you might be working or the people with whom you will be doing business. If covering up your tattoos will help you land and keep a job, then it's something you might want to consider. Perhaps it will become less of an issue once people have gotten to know you. If you have the mindset that you would prefer not to work for or with someone who has a problem with your tattoos, that is also your decision.

Lotion

OK . . remember the part where I said this could get uncomfortable. This is another one of those areas. If you are not familiar with the term "ashy," this might not register for you. You might find this bit of information funny if you're in a mixed group with a phenomenal facilitator! If you are familiar with the term ashy, then you know where I'm going. Put some lotion on so your hands, elbows, knees, etc., look well moisturized, and don't draw unnecessary attention.

The lotion rule goes for men and women. You are likely to end up shaking hands at some point. At the very least, you're going to be in close enough proximity to people that they will be able to see your hands. Be sure nails are cleaned and trimmed. If you wear nail polish, be sure it's neat.

Dental Hygiene

Perhaps you are afraid of the dentist. Or, you don't have dental insurance, you are embarrassed because your teeth are in bad condition, or you don't think about it because you don't seem to have any problems with your teeth or gums at the moment. If you have not had a dental exam for some time, let's see if we can get you to a place where you can change that.

If you already know some dental issues are going on, it's time to address them. What you can do on your own: Brush twice a day and floss once a day. Brushing and flossing are considered minimal and do not take that much time. Spend at least two minutes brushing your teeth, and remember to brush your gums, the roof of your mouth and your tongue. Yes, it would help if you brushed your tongue or used a tongue scraper. Brushing your teeth gets all of the easy to reach places in your mouth to prevent tartar build-up. Dental hygienists recommend flossing to complete your dental hygiene. This information from Matt Cunningham may help. Matt wrote an article entitled, "Five Reasons Why Flossing is Extremely Important." The five reasons are:

> I was once at the dentist and the dental assistants were all laughing about a client who had come in and was so afraid of the dentist, they described how he was clutching the arms of the chair and perspiring terribly. The staff though it was hysterical because the described him as being this man's man kinda guy. I laughed along as they continued talking about this patient who had been in the Marine Corp, the Army and had been a Philadelphia police officer. It was then that all the coincidences collided, and I said, "wait a minute . . . that sounds like my dad!" Yes, my dad was ridiculously afraid of the dentist. Still, as fearful as he was, he went anyway! And you need to go as well.

1. Flossing and brushing are more effective than brushing alone

2. Flossing protects your gums too (not just your teeth)

3. Flossing can save you money (preventative health saves money in the long run)

4. Flossing helps prevent other diseases

5. Flossing prevents tartar build-up (it gets to areas and does things that your toothbrush and mouth wash can't)

If you have dental insurance, pick up the phone and find out where to go for your dental exam. Make the appointment and handle your business. It probably won't be the most pleasant experience of your life, especially if you're afraid of the dentist.

If you do not have dental insurance. Contact a local social service agency to find out if you can get discounted or free dental services. And, look at local churches and other community agencies that offer free services. Some churches provide free services as a result of volunteers who donate their time and skills. Many people don't know about these opportunities because they don't investigate. It's time for you to explore your options.

If you aren't currently working, when you do get your next job, ask about dental insurance or a Flexible Spending Plan (FSA) that will allow you to set funds aside to go toward medical expenses like dental.

Well, you probably weren't expecting a section on hygiene, so let's move on to something a bit more fun. How about cosmetics and grooming products?! Men don't go anywhere. In this day and age, men are using hair color, wearing wigs and hairpieces, getting manicures, using under-eye concealer, and spending as much time "getting ready" as a woman might.

Fragrances and Colognes

Smells are a powerful aspect of life. Aromatherapy is an industry. You can probably think of a scent from your past that immediately takes you back to a childhood memory. It might be pleasant or unpleasant, but as soon as you recall it or smell something similar, you are transported back in time.

Do you have a memory associated with an aroma? It might be a pleasant or unpleasant smell from your past. If so, write it down.

_____

_____

_____

_____

Cosmetics

You do not have to wear cosmetics. If it doesn't feel right for you, don't do it. Applying make-up takes time. Having it and maintaining the products you use - takes money. Many women choose to wear cosmetics, and cosmetics can be worn with minimal financial investment. Do what works for you.

If you need assistance:

- Go to a professional.

- If going to the make-up counter at your local department store or drug store isn't possible, do your research on YouTube.

- Get a friend or family member to help you create a make-up style that works for you that you can eventually do on your own.

A straightforward regimen on clean, healthy skin might include mascara, under-eye concealer, brow pencil, and lip gloss.

Hair

There are tons of options for men and women regarding hair care, hairstyles and colors, and hair accessories. Learn about the culture at the places you interview. Find out if they have policies that don't align with how you want to show up. If you grow a beard after you get hired, is that going to be an issue? You should be able to wear your hair natural without it being an issue.

Are you familiar with the CROWN Act?

> The CROWN Act stands for "Creating a Respectful and Open World for Natural Hair," which prohibits race-based hair discrimination, which is the denial of employment and educational opportunities because of hair texture or protective hairstyles including braids, locks, twists, or Bantu knots. – thecrownact.com

Discrimination against men and women of African descent for wearing our hair in styles that celebrate its natural texture and cultural norms has been an issue for decades. Visit **www.thecrownact.com** to learn more about the CROWN Act.

Allergies

This isn't about *your* allergies. Although, you should be conscious of your allergies so you can speak to them when necessary. This is about people you come in contact with during your interview process and within work environments. I am allergic to coconut. That means a person who comes in to interview with me who is wearing coconut oil in their hair, on their body, etc., would create a problem for me without even being aware. This can be a sensitive subject for both parties.

What I hope you take away from this section is paying attention to your style, the work environment, your cultural norms, and the practicality of working around other people can create challenges.

Here are a few organizations that are in the business of helping people Get Ready to Work by providing clothing, accessories, and other support. Check your local listing and community agencies for chapters or organizations that offer similar services.

Agency	Website	Description
Career Gear	www.careergear.org	Career Gear empowers men entering or re-entering the workforce to look and feel their best by providing clothing that boosts their image.
Clothes the Deal	www.clothesthedeal.org	Offers low-income jobseekers a professional image so they are confident going into interview opportunities.
Dress for Success	www.dressforsuccess.org	Dress for Success is a global organization that helps empower women by providing them with resources, including professional attire for interviews.
Jails to Jobs	www.jailstojobs.org	Provides clothing and other resources for individuals re-entering the workforce after being incarcerated.
Ready for Success	www.readyforsuccessmn.org	Provides low-income men and women with gently used and new professional clothing, accessories and toiletries to prepare them for interviews and employment.

You can also check your local Salvation Army or Goodwill locations.

Social Media and Brand YOU!

Having a healthy social media presence is beneficial. Whether it is your profile on LinkedIn or your company website, know that the first thing many people will do after receiving your information is look for you on social media. And if you're thinking, *"Oh, my job isn't that important,"* or *"I'm just getting started with my career, so it doesn't matter,"* be aware that even your personal Facebook profile is subject to review by potential employers.

There are three questions I want you to consider as you review this section:

1. What does your online brand say about you?

2. What have you made available for people to view?

3. How can I best use one or more of these sites to my advantage?

Here are four social media sites you might want to become familiar with if you are not already.

LinkedIn

As of Jan 2020, LinkedIn boasted over 675 million members. LinkedIn is the largest online professional networking site in the world. You can use it for networking, job searches, and job postings. I believe LinkedIn provides the best opportunity for developing, maintaining, and growing your online professional network.

Visit LinkedIn and write down something you learned about the site?

_____

_____

_____

_____

Facebook Pages

Facebook Pages are different than Personal Profiles. It is necessary to have a Personal Profile to create a Professional Page. If you have a business, you should consider making a Facebook Page. Unlike a Personal Profile, which will only allow 5,000 Friends, a Page allows for unlimited followers. You can use your professional Page to run advertising and use Facebook's algorithms to track the data. Tracking algorithms is not possible on your personal Facebook Profile.

Visit Facebook and see if you can note the difference between Personal Profiles and Professional Pages. What do you see?

_____

_____

_____

_____

What are Facebook Stories?

_____

_____

_____

_____

What is Facebook Live?

_____

_____

_____

_____

Instagram

Instagram is a visual media app used on phones. You can post images, videos, and text, but it is primarily for visual posts. FYI: Facebook now owns Instagram.

Visit Instagram and write down what you liked or didn't like about how some people are using their Instagram accounts.

_____

_____

_____

_____

What is IGTV?

_____

_____

_____

_____

Twitter

Twitter is a social media platform used primarily for posting text messages. It does allow for images and video links.

Visit Twitter and write down what you did and didn't like about Twitter.

_____

_____

_____

_____

YouTube

Video based social media platform. Requires consistent content to grow and sustain an audience. YouTube has ad selling capabilities. Provides a location to store videos that can be embedded on websites or shared on other social media sites.

Do you watch videos on YouTube? If so, what are some of your favorite things to watch on YouTube?

_____

_____

_____

_____

Do you have a YouTube Channel? If so, what do you show on it; if not, what would you show on a YouTube Channel if you had one?

_____

_____

_____

_____

These are basic descriptions for five popular social media sites or apps one might use for professional purposes. There are many more. There are tutorials available if you want to learn how to use these applications more efficiently. Social media professionals charge varying fees to teach people how to use these sites. Other professionals offer their services to help manage sites on behalf of professionals who can afford it and do not have the time to do it themselves.

Social Media Warnings

Never pay for Likes or Followers! Some services offer to increase the Likes and Followers on social media sites. Buying Likes and Followers is not recommended. Doing this creates the appearance of interests, but they don't generate authentic engagement on your Page because they aren't real. It's never good to have a professional Page that appears to have disengaged Followers. And if that isn't bad enough, when sites like Facebook take notice, you risk having your account deleted.

Use Privacy and Security Settings. If you have personal accounts on any of these sites, learn how to access the privacy settings so you can set the parameters that give you more control over who has access to your personal information.

Respect Copyrights. If you are using photographs, videos, or music that belong to someone else, legally, you are supposed to get written permission to use them especially, when using it for professional purposes. If you write, "I do not have the rights to this music," or "I do not own this song," that does not mean you have permission to use it. What are your options? Look for pictures and music listed as Royalty-Free. That means you have the right to use it without having to pay the owner a royalty fee for usage. You may have to pay to download the music, but you don't have to continue to pay a royalty or recurring fee to the owner.

These are a few sites that offer royalty-free pictures or music.

Resources

Website	Description
www.unsplash.com	Royalty free, free photos
www.freemusicarchive.org	Royalty free music, free music
www.premiumbeat.com	Royalty free music

Public Speaking

I acknowledge that it is pretty challenging teaching the intricacies of public speaking from a Workbook. Still, I am confident that if you practice and apply what you learn here, you can improve the comfort level with which you operate when you do speak. You can empower yourself by finding multiple ways to improve as a speaker.

According to the National Institute of Health, 73% of the population suffers from glossophobia, which is the fear of public speaking. Anxiety over public speaking makes it the most common phobia ahead of death, spiders, and the fear of heights. We are so concerned about others' negative evaluations that it is considered a social anxiety disorder.

If this is you, know that the anxiety around speaking in public does not have to immobilize and silence you moving forward! As with most things, even if you still have butterflies, you can get better with practice. Having a little fear or nervousness about something does not mean you can't conquer the fear and become a good speaker.

Did you know what Barbra Streisand, Adele, Salma Hayek, Justin Timberlake, and many other famous people have in common? They have admitted to having stage fright or suffering from a social anxiety disorder. One of the most sought-after motivational speakers of the past 25 years, stuttered as a child and was told that he had a learning disability? Les Brown stuttered and was labeled learning disabled. He refused to allow either, to prevent him from becoming an impactful, world-renown motivational speaker.

As a child, I was shy. I was always watching and listening to other people. Even when I was singing into hairbrushes and talking aloud to myself, it would have never occurred to me that I would be an instructor, facilitator and public speaker who made a living standing in front of groups of people one day.

In this section, you will prepare a way of introducing yourself that equips others in your network to help you by way of referrals. We will also explore something Lisa Nichol's calls the SNAAP.

What have your experiences been up until now?

Have you ever had the opportunity to speak in front of a group?

☐ Yes ☐ No

What was the occasion?

_____

_____

_____

_____

What were you there to speak about?

_____

_____

_____

_____

Where were you?

_____

_____

_____

_____

How many people were there?

_____

_____

_____

_____

On the scale below, circle your level of nervousness or fear:

1   Perfectly fine

2   A little nervous, but mostly excitement

3   Nervous

4   Really nervous

5   Trembling with fear

How much preparation did you put into the presentation?

Hours   Minutes

_____   _____

Did you write down what you were going to say?

☐ Yes ☐ No

Did you have notes or slides with you during the presentation?

☐ Yes ☐ No

Did you celebrate getting through it!?

☐ Yes ☐ No

After the presentation, did you review the experience to assess what went well and what did not?

How did you think you did?

_____

_____

_____

What could you have done better?

_____

_____

_____

_____

What would you do differently next time?

_____

_____

_____

_____

Preparation

It is difficult to over prepare. I was an athlete all through high school and college. I relied on what I learned as an athlete to help me adjust to becoming a professional actor. As an athlete, everything that happened on the track field or the court happened because of the practice I put in as an individual and the work we did as a team. As a professional actor, it was the same thing. By the time we performed a live theatre production, we had put in hundreds of hours of rehearsal individually and as an ensemble.

Let's start with your introduction. How do you currently introduce yourself?

_____

_____

_____

_____

Do you introduce yourself differently in different settings?

☐ Yes ☐ No

If you chose "yes," how so?

_____

_____

_____

_____

Practicing is what will help you create a way to introduce yourself in professional situations. Know when it's appropriate to give your name and when it makes sense to include what you do and the type of assistance you need. Below are some examples.

Referral Request Example

This skill is excellent when you want to be introduced to someone who can help you find something or someone. If you are looking for a particular type of job, training, an employee you want to hire, or even a specific type of client you want for your business, learning to ask for a referral is great.

> Hi, I'm Jared Kettles, and I am currently in a job readiness program to prepare for interviews. I recently received my certificate in Microsoft office products, and I'm looking for a position working in the IT department in higher education. If you know anyone in that area, I would appreciate a connection that would allow me the opportunity to speak with them.

The key to this introduction is telling who you are, what you do, and how the listener can help. The benefit of this introduction is it immediately positions people to assist you if they are able and willing.

SNAAP – Super Networking at Accelerated Pace (as learned from Lisa Nichols)

A SNAAP is slightly different. A SNAAP is excellent in networking environments and in situations where you have the opportunity to share what it is that you do and who you help. It speaks to the solutions you have helped people find. Every businessperson should have a SNAAP that speaks to the services provided to their clients. Here's an example?

> As a result of putting into action what they learned in my clutter cleanse program, students and clients have transformed chaotic rooms in their homes into
>
> - beautiful kitchens where they're inspired to cook
> - home offices that have made working easier
> - spa-like bathrooms where they can relax, and
> - spacious walk-in closets where everything has a place
>
> They are all experiencing the joy of having relaxing and rejuvenating spaces in their home where NOW they love to live!
>
> I'm looking for people ready to up-level their living spaces and lives because they understand that transformation includes transforming the areas where they live. Who do you know?

The key to the SNAAP is it tells what you do by speaking about you helped clients. It paints a picture people can envision stepping into themselves.

Prepare! No matter how good you think you are at winging it or going off the top of your head, nothing beats practice. It is not an option, and it proves that you are invested in being an active participant in your success. I hope you always desire to manage the *controllables*. There will be plenty of things to happen that will be out of your control and somethings for which you could not have planned. The goal is to be confident enough in what you are aware of that you believe you can handle anything else that comes up.

How to Practice

1. Say your SNAAP or your Introduction into a mirror.

2. Practice using a recorder and playing it back so you can hear yourself.

3. Practice using a video recorder, hear and see yourself. Notice any distracting habits

4. Practice saying it to a friend or family member.

5. If you are in a class, make this a daily activity at the start of the course.

6. Use your Facebook, Zoom, , or another live feature to practice with someone online.

Watch others speak. TED and TEDx Talks are a great source of short talks to study. Pay attention to what you like, what you don't like, and why. How do speakers use humor? How do they keep your attention?

Practice your Introduction, SNAAP, or both – several times:

Introduction

#1

_____

_____

_____

_____

#2

_____

_____

_____

_____

SNAAP

#1

_____

_____

_____

_____

#2

_____

_____

_____

_____

#3

_____

_____

_____

_____

Relationship Building or Networking

It is estimated that 65% to 75% of jobs are obtained through relationships or what is referred to as networking. Maybe you are familiar with the many networking groups, organizations, and online social media sites telling you how networking can benefit you in your career development. And still, you may have no idea how to begin networking.

First, what is professional networking? Networking is work. Some treat it as a passive activity, while others have made it an intentional aspect of their professional development. I will preface my definition by saying this; there are many variations on this theme. After many years of involvement in various networking organizations, this has come to be my definition.

> Professional networking or business networking is the intentional process of developing and maintaining profitable relationships to exchange useful information and resources that benefit individuals professionally. In this case, profitability may include financial increase, access to resources, being a resource, or gaining knowledge.

What networking is not: It is not a lopsided relationship designed to provide a one-way stream of resources to the person looking for a job. In other words, networking is not an "all about you" venture, simply because you may be the person in search of employment. Even if you are unemployed, your attitude should be, "What do I have to offer?" The following exercises are designed to help you be confident that you can be a valuable asset when networking.

Assessing Your Contacts

Networking is not a numbers game. It is about the quality of the relationships you develop, and it requires practice. Begin with those closest to you. Depending upon where you are in your career, you may not have many *professional* relationships to work with, and that is fine. Work with what you have now. Look at the contacts in your Outlook, your Rolodex, or wherever you keep your contact list! As you go through them, divide them into three groups based upon your relationship with each individual. Here are the three categories (feel free to rename them):

- **Valuable:** Meaning people with whom you have done business; have established a strong positive relationship; and individuals who would likely be comfortable recommending you should an opportunity present itself.

- **Accessible:** Meaning someone you communicate with, but your relationship has not developed to one where you have done business with them; or where you know enough about each other to be comfortable making a referral.

- **Visible:** Meaning you and this person may or may not recognize each other on-site, but there is no real relationship established beyond that.

The remaining contacts are individuals with whom you have no identifiable relationship, beyond the fact, at some point, you obtained their information. These are the deletes, trash. Remember, this is not a numbers game. Having a massive list of contacts with whom you have no relationship serves no purpose in your new intentional professional networking and relationship development plan. Contacting them could be counterproductive to your goal of building relationships. If you are still gasping for air, you have permission, for now, to separate these contacts from the rest of your list.

Now you have a definition of professional networking. Feel free to tweak it and personalize it as you see fit. You also have your contact list sorted into three categorized groups and a delete pile. If you don't have much of a contact list to begin with, that's alright. You are now prepared to categorize once it starts growing.

If you run a business and use something like Constant Contact to maintain and organize your contacts, you may categorize contacts based upon the products and services they have purchased. Make the adjustments as needed. The key is that you are only spending time connecting with people who are interested in your offering.

Do the Work

Below are five things I would suggest you do before you officially begin entering networking forums:

1. Get business cards. Be professional.

It is a misnomer to think you only need business cards when you are employed. They can be even more beneficial when you are not working. Keep them simple, name, email, telephone, and your status as a student (program/degree). If you are looking for work, you can include the type of work that you do. If you order cards with no gloss, you will be able to write on them. This is great if you need to write additional information on the back. It is also great if you meet someone who does not have a business card with them, you can put their info on the card's back for follow up. You can visit your local office supply store or go online to a service like Visitaprint.com.

2. Create an online Signature. Be savvy.

Business cards are great, but what about working online? Consider how much business communication is happening via email these days? For this reason, consider creating an email signature you can use when sending out professional emails. Whatever email service you are using, it more than likely has a way for you to create a signature. A signature shows up at the end of your email and provides your name, title, contact information, and if you have one, a company logo or website link. Check with your provider and learn how you can create an email signature.

3. Have a current resume. Be prepared.

If you can keep a clean, up-to-date documents or couple of copies of your resume with you when you're out and about, that would be awesome. At best, be sure you have clean, up-to-date copies on hand, and the same resume in a digital format, so it's available to send as an attachment. The information in your LinkedIn or other social media profiles should be consistent with what is on your resume. Find a professional to do or at the very least review your resume.

4. Make a statement. Be polished

Be able to verbalize (in 30 to 60 seconds) who you are, what you do now, what you are looking to do, or with whom you are looking to connect. Example: "I spent five years working as a medic in the Navy. I am currently completing my BSHSA degree, and I am interested in networking with others currently working in healthcare administration."

5. Research networking forums. Be proactive.

Do your homework. Learn what groups are out there and who is involved with them. The newspaper, library, chamber of commerce, and online searches can help you identify networking groups and organizations in your area.

The online site MeetUp offers opportunities to associate with like-minded people around a variety of topics and activities. Online is a great place to look for networking groups that align with everything from hobbies you might have to professional interests.

If this is beginning to feel like work, you are on the right path. After all, it is netWORKing. And you are now on your way to making it work for you.

If you are reading this book as part of a course or an online program, you can begin with others taking the course with you. Practice your introductions and your SNAAPs, and start finding your networking partners. Who can you refer to someone, and who can direct you? Who has a service or product you are interested in, and who is interested in yours? Be mindful not to spend time trying to "sell" the people around you. That becomes annoying fast. This is about practicing what you've learned and allowing natural connections to be made.

Always seek to be of service. In other words, the power of networking is in the potential for it to be mutually beneficial. Active relationship building is how the wonderful web of professional networking grows and grows and grows. Sometimes it is for your benefit, and other times you will be the one adding value to someone else's situation. It is your responsibility to ask questions to find out how you can be of service to others.

Interviewing

Some say that life often gives you second chances. I would almost guarantee you that this rarely applies when it comes to interviews. With an interview, you would be much better off remembering, "You get one chance to make a good first impression."

In this section, you will learn to:

- Create a list of items and information needed before, during, and after the interview

- Identify when each item gets used or presented

- Discuss the importance of the things and information

- Identify what tools you are missing or require

- Answer the question: How do I feel now compared to how I felt before completing this section?

> Planning is bringing the future into the present so that you can do something about it now.
>
> ~ Alan Lakein

The Purpose of an Interview

An interview is your opportunity to make the best presentation possible to the hiring manager or team. Various types of interviews are reviewed in the upcoming section. Remember, the interview is one of those first impression opportunities. But your best self forward. Trust the process. Interviewing can be stressful, exciting, anxiety-ridden, and rewarding. It's often about how you look at the opportunity and how well you have prepared for the experience.

Finally, I like to share that the interview is a two-way street. Not only are you being interviewed for a position, but you are also interviewing. People turn down job opportunities all the time after going through the interview process and deciding; the right answer is "No, thank you."

What are some of the reasons you think people might turn down a job offer after completing the interview process?

_____

_____

_____

_____

Face-to-Face Interviews are the ones with which most people are familiar. Face-to-Face interviews usually occur when you, the candidate, travel to a location to meet with someone involved in the hiring process. The meeting often takes place on-site at the company doing the hiring.

Have you ever had a face-to-face interview?

☐ Yes ☐ No

What did you like about it?

_____

_____

_____

_____

Did anything make you nervous? If so, what? Why?

_____

_____

_____

_____

Dining Interviews happen over a meal. They could happen over breakfast, lunch, or dinner and your best bet is to eat beforehand. If you are invited to an interview like this, always remember to keep it professional. No alcohol. Mind your table manners. If this means you need to get coaching before going to a lunch interview on what utensils to use – then do so.

What do you think some of the challenges of this type of interview could be?

_____

_____

_____

_____

Online or Video Interviews. These could be live interviews using Skype, OoVoo, Facetime, or other live, internet-based video conferencing. Treat this interview the same way you would treat any other face-to-face interview by being prepared and appropriately dressed.

Live Streaming Interview. One of my nieces is an on-air news anchor. One of the interviews during the interview process was a video interview. There was a time when these types of interviews were rare. Today, with technology and living through the pandemic, online interviews, like meetings, are happening more frequently.

Pre-recorded. Pre-recorded interviews require that you record yourself in advance. You may be asked to record it using your equipment.

When having an online or recorded interview, the location is relevant. You want the area you will record in to be private, quiet, clean, and well lit. You want to be sure no one is walking around behind you while recording or being interviewed. You want to eliminate as much background noise as possible. Be sure the areas behind and around you are clutter-free. You do not want the person interviewing you to be distracted by piles of laundry, dishes, your unmade bed, or other signs of disarray. And finally, face a light source, so you are well lit during the interview.

Go online and look up how to set up a successful video. You may need to make a small investment to get a clip-on microphone and a light. Those two things can make an enormous difference.

Telephone Interviews and even the call you receive to set-up a face-to-face interview should be handled with the same attention to detail as the interview. Again, be sure you are in a location that will give you the privacy you need to have the conversation. Be prepared with any documents or notes you might want to have during your call. Be prepared to take notes and have any questions you've thought of in advance ready to go. And, smile! If you need to keep a small mirror near your work area so you can see yourself smiling, do it. It makes a difference in the tone of your voice.

Group Interviews are interviews where several candidates get interviewed at once. Group interviews may sound confusing, and it can sometimes be awkward because candidates feel as though they are in direct competition with one another. Keep in mind that although you may be interviewing for the same position as other applicants in the room, you may also be required to work together after getting hired. Do not allow someone else's lack of professionalism to throw you off course. Your goal is to be courteous, focused, and professional so they see you presenting your best self throughout the entire process.

Panel Interviews are interviews where several people interview one candidate at the same time. Now, where the group interview can sometimes breed competition, the panel interview can sometimes heighten insecurities! In can be intimidated having two or more people asking you questions. The good news is you only have to answer one question at a time. Stay calm and do not allow yourself to become overwhelmed. You may pick up on distinctive personality types amongst the panel members; do not let that throw you. Be pleasant. This may be an excellent time to use your character strengths to stay engaged. Focus on the questions. Thank about your answers before responding. Maintain natural eye contact.

Staffing Firm or Temp Agency Interviews. Here you will interview with someone from an agency paid to help place you in a position. Staffing means they help a company find staff, i.e., employees, to fill open positions within the organization. Temp is short for temporary and refers to employees hired to fill open positions, usually for a defined period. It may be while they search for a permanent employee or while a full-time employee is on leave.

You may be more likely to use temp agency services early in your career. Later, once you have established yourself as a skilled professional or high-level executive, you may enlist the services of a recruiting firm that you pay to help find you employment. I will be discussing agencies hired by companies to find candidates.

Your interview process with a staffing firm could involve several different types of interviews already mentioned. You may be required to have a short telephone interview before they invite you into the office. If the staffing agency only sees candidates on certain days, you may be invited to participate in a group interview with other potential candidates.

Another aspect of many staffing firm or temp agency interview processes includes skill assessments. If the agency representative believes you are a suitable candidate, you may be invited to complete one or more assessments. Assessments can determine your skill level in basic word processing knowledge, math skills, reading, writing, word comprehension, etc. The results allow the agency to determine what positions you are best suited for based upon their client's work order and what salary range they can command for your services.

The good thing about meeting with and working with a staffing or temp agency is that they often become your advocate. If you interview well and present yourself well, you can become a candidate they work hard to place in a position with one of their clients. And, when that assignment is over, they will be eager to place you with another client because they know they can depend on you to do a great job. The assessments are beneficial because they allow you to identify your strengths and the areas that show opportunity for improvement.

Another benefit of temp positions is they allow you to learn about different organizations. It is not uncommon that temp employees are offered full-time jobs when they come open because the company has gotten to know your skillset and work ethic.

Notes

_____

_____

_____

_____

Information and Documents

This is information you should have prepared before you interview. Completing this information will also help you prepare for creating your resume.

Complete Your Identification and Contact Information

Legal Name

First Name: _____ Middle Name: _____

Last Name: _____

Birthdate: _____ Height: _____ Weight: _____

Let's discuss:

- Nickname – a name you're called by family and friends.`

- Maiden name

- Surname

- Other

Street Address: _____

City: _____ State: _____ Zip: _____

Cell: _____ Home: _____ Fax: _____

Email: _____

Let's discuss:

- Home Address

- Mailing Address

- P.O. Box

- Professional email addresses

Complete Your Employment / Volunteer History

Name of Employer: _____

Street Address: _____

City: _____ State: _____ Zip: _____

Your Job Title: _____

Name of Supervisor: _____ Telephone: _____

Date Job Started: _____ Date Job Ended: _____

Duties, Responsibilities, Achievements:

1. _____

2. _____

3. _____

Name of Employer: _____

Street Address: _____

City: _____ State: _____ Zip: _____

Your Job Title: _____

Name of Supervisor: _____ Telephone: _____

Date Job Started: _____ Date Job Ended: _____

Duties, Responsibilities, Achievements:

1. _____

2. _____

3. _____

Complete Your Education and / or Training History

Name of High School: _____

Street Address: _____

City: _____ State: _____ Zip: _____

Did you graduate? ☐ Yes ☐ No

If yes, did you receive a: ☐ GED ☐ Diploma

Graduation Date: _____

Honors / Awards:

_____

_____

Name of School / College / University: _____

Street Address: _____

City: _____ State: _____ Zip: _____

Did you graduate? ☐ Yes ☐ No

If "yes," graduation date: _____ Degree Earned: _____

Honors / Awards:

_____

_____

Name of School / College / University: _____

Street Address: _____

City: _____   State: _____   Zip: _____

Did you graduate? ☐ Yes ☐ No

If "yes," graduation date:_____   Degree Earned: _____

Honors / Awards:

_____

_____

Name of School / College / University: _____

Street Address: _____

City: _____   State: _____   Zip: _____

Did you graduate? ☐ Yes ☐ No

If "yes," graduation date:_____   Degree Earned: _____

Honors / Awards:

_____

_____

Name of School / College / University: _____

Street Address: _____

City: _____   State: _____   Zip: _____

Did you graduate? ☐ Yes ☐ No

If "yes," graduation date:_____   Degree Earned: _____

Honors / Awards:

_____

_____

Proof of Citizenship and Proof of Identification

Birth Certificate

According to the American Bar Association, a birth certificate is a document issued by a government that records the birth of a child for vital statistics, tax, military, and census purposes,

There are several reasons when you might be required to show your birth certificate. One reason is if you need to obtain or replace your social security card. This is important because almost every job application or onboarding documentation will ask for your social security number.

Contact the Clerk of Records or County Clerk Office in your municipality to determine where and how you can obtain a copy of your birth certificate. There is usually a fee, so be sure to ask about the fee and how you can pay. You may be able to request it online.

Passport

A passport is a travel document, usually issued by a country's government to its citizens. It is necessary for international travel. A passport is also considered acceptable proof of ID for employment purposes.

You can apply for a passport by going to **www.travel.state.gov**. Some Post Offices and drug stores are equipped to take passport photos. You can obtain the passport application at most Post Office locations as well. Passport photos can also be taken at some pharmacies. There is an application fee that is paid to the U.S. Passport office. There is no fee to complete or submit the documents if you do it yourself. Be careful that you are on the U.S. government's official travel site to obtain the documents.

Social Security (Number) Card

The Social Security Administration issues social security numbers. Your nine-digit social security number is what connects you to the Social Security Administration.

You can use your Social Security Number for identification. It is required so your covered wages are accurately recorded. That includes self-employment earnings. Your Social Security Number also helps SSA monitor and record your Social Security benefits once they begin. You will need a social security number to be employed.

To obtain a Social Security Number (card) or to replace a lost Social Security card, you should contact the Social Security Administration at **www.ssa.gov**. Beware of social security scams. If your Social Security Number has been lost or stolen, report it immediately to SSA.

Employer Identification Number (EIN) or Federal Employer Identification Number (FEIN)

A FEIN / EIN is issued to business entities operating in the United States. It is issued by the Internal Revenue Services (IRS) as a form of identification.

If you are doing work under your business, you will use your FEIN / EIN in a similar way an individual would use a Social Security Number.

Contact the IRS at **www.irs.gov** for information on how to apply for an EIN. Again, be sure you are on the IRS official site.

EINs do not expire.

Driver's License

The State issues a driver's license as proof of an individual's legal right to operate a vehicle. A driver's license can also be used as a form of ID for employment purposes.

To obtain a driver's license for the first time, contact the Division or Department of Motor Vehicles (DMV) in your State for information. If you currently have a license, be sure it is current. If your license is ever lost or stolen, report it immediately.

State Identification (ID)

Some states issue State Identification Cards that look similar to a driver's license. State identification cards verify a person's birth date and legal presence.

A State ID can be used for identification purposes, as it verifies the same identification information as a driver's license. DMV can also issue an identification card. A State ID does NOT authorize you to drive a vehicle.

References – Personal and Professional

What is a reference?

A professional reference is someone who can talk about your work experience, character, skills, and work habits. A personal reference is someone who can talk about aspects of your personality, character, or life that may be of particular importance to a potential employer.

Why might you need a reference?

As part of the job search process, you may be asked to provide a list of references.

What do potential employers discuss with references?

Some questions an interviewer might ask personal or professional reference include:

- What was it like working with Jared?

- How would you describe Shawn's ability to handle challenges?

    - Can you give me an example?

- What were Yvette's strengths as a manager?

- What areas did Jon have room for growth?

- Would you hire Jane again if given the opportunity?

Who can be a reference?

Select your references carefully. Do not pick references because they have what appears to be an essential title or position, if:

- They don't know you well enough to give you a favorable reference.

- You did not have a good working relationship with them.

- They aren't familiar with what you did as an employee.

Do I need to ask the person in advance? YES!

Always check with people you want to use as a reference BEFORE you provide their information. Always check with your selected references anytime you provide their information to an employer. You want your references to be aware and prepared should they be called.

What information should I get from a reference?

Once you've identified someone as a potential reference, you want to call and ask if it's alright that you use them. Then you want to get the following:

- Full name (Mr. Ms. Mrs. Dr.)

- Current job title / Employer

- The best telephone number where they can be reached

- Email address

- Mailing address

What information should I give my references to prepare them?

Once you have been asked for your list of references, contact your references immediately to let them know to expect to receive communication from:

- Name of the person who will be calling

- The Company they are calling from

- The position for which you applied

    o It is best if you can send them the complete job description

The is a great time to have a conversation or send an email to your reference, providing them with two to three things that would be beneficial for them to cover during the reference call.

For example:

If it is a leadership position where you will be managing a team, you might ask your reference to be sure and discuss something that demonstrates your ability to lead a team.

There may be a time when you apply for a position that is a growth position. In other words, the position is slightly beyond your work experience. If that happens, you want to help your reference by coaching them to speak to times that show how well you learn, how teachable or coachable you are, or how you took the initiative to learn so you could excel in that role.

When to Provide References?

Only give references when asked, which means do not list your references on your resume.

There are several reasons why I recommend this.

First, if one of your reference's changes jobs, or telephone numbers, or their title changes in between your interview process, you may be providing incorrect contact information.

Second, it allows you the opportunity to contact your references for this specific job when you need them. You will confirm that the information you have for them is still accurate and give them the information they will need about the position. A prepared reference is your best reference.

Avoid Reference Fatigue

If you are interviewing often, you want to avoid having anyone feel like they are being overwhelmed by calls from potential employers. Also, consider that you may not be the only person using your reference as a reference; And they might have busy schedules to navigate.

If you put together a list of five or six professional references, you will have enough people to rotate. Then, you will be prepared if one or two references becomes unavailable.

Resume – Your Story to Show & Tell

Now you have all the information you need to create a resume. Be aware that this information will change over time, and it is your responsibility to be sure that your resume stays current and accurate. Information on your resume should be truthful, and you must be able to substantiate it. That means, include what is true and be able to back it up with proof! Here's a story to help you better understand what this means and why it is crucial.

Learning Scenario

Mrs. Harris was judging contestants in a local pageant. All of the contestants were in high school, and they were all accomplished academically. Their resumes indicated that these young ladies were involved in various activities and affiliated with many clubs and organizations. Mrs. Harris noticed that a good portion of the contestants listed membership in foreign language clubs at their high schools. Some contestants held officer positions in their foreign language clubs, and others had been members for two, three, and even four years. A few young ladies even mentioned that they had gone on international trips to Mexico, French, and Italy, due to their involvement in these foreign language clubs.

So, it should not have been a surprise, during the interviews, whenever Mrs. Harris would see a foreign language club affiliation on a contestant's resume, she would ask the contestant to say something to her in the language identified. Time and time again, Mrs. Harris was greeted with a startling blank stare. Some contestants were "saved by the timer" and had to move to the next judge's interview station before they could answer. Others stammered that they couldn't think on such short notice. A few started but could not get through a full sentence in the foreign language they had been studying.

Mrs. Harris was not sure what to make of this information.

Would you say not being able to speak the foreign language helped, hurt, or had no effect on their interview?

_____

_____

_____

_____

What might Mrs. Harris be thinking about the contestants who could not speak a foreign language – even though it...

_____

_____

_____

_____

Review activities, interests, hobbies, skills, etc., on your resume, and be sure you are confident and prepared to discuss this information in your interview. One way to prepare is to have examples of experiences.

If you indicate that you are proficient in something a language, software program, or app, be prepared to demonstrate your aptitude, provide examples of how you have used it in the past, and provide certifications or proof of proficiency whenever possible.

RESUME TIPS

If you have completed the information section, you should have all of the vital information needed to create a resume. This section will give you some tips, tricks, and suggestions on getting your resume completed or updated.

Who Should Do Your Resume And Why

I recommend that you find a skilled resume writer to be sure the final document represents you well in every way possible. You already know how important it is for the information to be correct and accurate. You also want your resume formatted adequately and free of grammatical errors. Another important aspect is for it to be written with the specific position in mind, whenever possible.

Keywords

A resume writer will also be familiar with things like keywords. Resume keywords are words and phrases that relate to a specific job description. Using keywords means your resume may need to be adjusted to include keywords related to a particular position, using keywords and phrases from the job description. This is important because whether it's a person or an automatic tracking system (ATS) that scans your resume, you want the person or the system to pick up words and phrases that help your resume stand out.

Formatting and Length

By reviewing sample resumes, you can get familiar with the different ways resumes are formatted. Sometimes they are formatted based on experience or the type of work. People in higher education often have resumes called CVs. CV stands for curriculum vitae, which is Latin for "course of life." CVs can be several pages in length. If you are not in higher education, you will likely never use a CV. Resumes are generally one to two pages in length and provide a chronological outline of work experience and education. Someone who does not have a lot of work experience might have their resume formatted differently than a person with years of experience.

Have fun researching different resume layouts. There are many ways to access different resume layouts and templates. Microsoft Word has resume templates available to use. When you open a NEW DOCUMENT> select FILE >, NEW FROM TEMPLATE, the template file will open. From there, you can search for RESUMES. You will see dozens of resume templates. You can also Google resume layouts or resume templates.

Affordable Resume Writer

Resume services can cost hundreds of dollars. An inexpensive option is to visit sites like www.upwork.com or www.fiverr.com, where you can hire contractors for jobs on an as needed basis and often save a considerable amount of money. If you decide to do it yourself or have a willing friend or family member work with you to complete your resume, considering hiring someone to proof-read it for you to be sure your resume is as good as it can be.

What key take-aways do you have from this section on resumes? Do you need a resume? Does yours need to be updated? Where will you go to get started?

_____

_____

Interview Prep Sheet

Here is a list to help you prepare for each interview.

Position (Title) Applied for: _____

Company Name: _____

Company Address: _____

Contact Person at Company (Name / Title): _____

Contact Person's Number: _____

Contact Person's Email: _____

The name and titles of everyone you will interview with:

Name / Title: _____

Name / Title: _____

Name / Title: _____

What type of interview:

☐ Online ☐ Video ☐ Telephone ☐ Other

Research

What have you learned about the company that you like?

What does the company do or produce?

_____

_____

_____

_____

Who are their clients?

_____

_____

_____

_____

Who is the competition?

_____

_____

_____

_____

Remember when I said interviews go both ways? Well, you should also try to learn something about the people or person who will be interviewing you.

Visit the company website and see what you can learn about the person(s) who will interview you?

_____

_____

_____

_____

What do you know about the position? (Be sure to have a copy of the job description that you have reviewed thoroughly.)

_____

_____

_____

_____

Why do you feel you're a good fit for this position? Provide examples:

Skills

_____

_____

_____

Experience

_____

_____

_____

Education

_____

_____

_____

Passion / Interest / Purpose

_____

_____

_____

If this is your first time applying for a position like this, be able to share other experiences that demonstrate how you have:

Learned New Things

_____

_____

_____

_____

Excelled in Situations in the Past

_____

_____

_____

_____

Demonstrated Commitment

_____

_____

_____

_____

Demonstrated Competence

_____

_____

_____

_____

Interview Preparation Checklist

Task	Check
Do you need childcare?	
Transportation to interview?	
Test run to location completed?	
Resume on-hand?	
References have been identified?	
You have contacted references?	
You know what you are wearing?	
Hair, makeup, accessories set?	
Notepad for interview	

During the Interview

Have questions prepared.

If you have an agency representative, they should have already told you the salary range.

If you are not working through an agency, you will need to find out. You can ask, "What is the salary range for this position?"

The initial interview isn't the time to negotiate. It is always good to have certain information. What have you learned about the position before the interview?

_____

_____

_____

_____

If you are working with an agency, the agency representative will be the one negotiating your salary. If it comes up during your interview, you should probably refer that discussion to your agency representative and let them handle it. That is part of what they are skilled at doing, so let them do their job.

After the Interview

Be prepared to send a thank you Note, Letter, Card - Mailed or Emailed - to:

- People or Head person where you interviewed

- Your representative at the agency if they set up the interview

- Your references who were called

_____

_____

_____

_____

When You Get a Job Offer

Be ready to negotiate. Have a dignified discussion about your salary. That means, know the salary range of the position and where your skills and intangible assets place you on the pay scale.

_____

_____

_____

_____

When You Get Hired

Celebrate! And be sure to contact your references and share the good news.

Now is a great time to send another card. Be creative! Maybe, after you've received one or two paychecks, you set up times to take each of them for coffee. Nothing expensive. Do what you can afford.

If You Do Not Get the Job Offer

How are you feeling?

It's okay to feel whatever you are feeling. Write it down:

_____

_____

_____

_____

_____

_____

_____

Review the Experience

What do you think you could have done to have improved your interview experience?

_____

_____

_____

_____

_____

_____

_____

Grow from the Opportunity

If it's possible, speak with the person who interviewed you, or ask your agency representative to ask if there was anything you could have done to improve your chances of getting offered the position.

_____

_____

_____

_____

_____

_____

_____

Move On

Any information you receive could be valuable in helping you be better prepared for your next interview. What can you use moving forward?

_____

_____

_____

_____

_____

_____

GREAT WORK!

Congratulations on completing your Get Ready to Work Workbook.

For a way to celebrate the good things happening in your life each day, check out my "What Went Well? Journals" for Adults, Couples, and Kids! Learn more by visiting www.liveempoweredinstitute.com.

Made in the USA
Monee, IL
18 April 2021